How to Generate and Earn Royalty Income

Marina Peters

Follow Marina Peters on

marinapetersbooks.com

to get updates on the latest projects

and see her other books.

How to Generate and Earn Royalty Income

From casual side income

to a

new investment category

Marina Peters

Copyright © 2020

© 2020 Marina Peters

Independently published

ISBN: 979-8-625206853

Disclaimer

All knowledge contained in this book is given for informational and educational purposes only. The author is not in any way accountable for any results or outcomes that emanate from using this material. Constructive attempts have been made to provide information that is both accurate and effective, but the author is not bound for the accuracy or use/misuse of this information.

The information herein is offered for informational purposes solely, and is universal as so. The presentation of the information is without contract or any type of guarantee assurance.

This book does not have the intention to be academically correct and it has been written in a casual style. I just want to provide the reader with my collected experience, information and consolidated knowledge on the topic without having an academic approach. This book is a complete private project. There is no connection whatsoever to a former or current employer.

In no way is it legal to reproduce, duplicate, or transmit any part of this document in either electronic means or in printed format. Recording of this publication is strictly prohibited and any storage of this document is not allowed unless with written permission from the publisher. All rights reserved.

The information provided herein is stated to be truthful and consistent, in that any liability, in terms of inattention or otherwise, by any usage or abuse of any policies, processes, or directions contained within is the solitary and utter responsibility of the recipient reader. Under no circumstances will any legal responsibility or blame be held against the publisher for any reparation, damages, or monetary loss due to the information herein, either directly or indirectly.

The trademarks that are used are without any consent, and the publication of the trademark is without permission or backing by the trademark owner. All trademarks and brands within this book are for clarifying purposes only and are the owned by the owners themselves, not affiliated with this document.

CONTENT

1	**INTRODUCTION**	**8**
1.1	Overview	8
1.2	Why are royalty payments important?	10
2	**WHAT ARE ROYALTIES?**	**12**
2.1	Definition	12
2.2	Types of Royalty Agreements	14
3	**DIFFERENT INDUSTRIES THAT PAY ROYALTIES**	**17**
3.1	Music Industry	17
3.2	Oil and gas Industry	19
3.3	Patents	21
3.4	Art	24
3.5	Photos	26
3.6	Trademarks	27
3.7	Software	28
3.8	Fashion	30
3.9	Book publishing	32
3.10	Television	34
4	**ROYALTY AGREEMENT TIPS FOR LICENSEES AND LICENSORS**	**35**

- 4.1 General 35
- 4.2 Royalty contracts 36
- 4.3 Conditions for terminating a royalty agreement 36
- 4.4 A case of an agreement termination 37
  - 4.4.1 General 37
  - 4.4.2 Options available 38
  - 4.4.3 Justifying the termination 38
  - 4.4.4 Comparison 39
  - 4.4.5 Consequences of the wrong termination 39
  - 4.4.6 Solution 39
- 4.5 Royalty Income 40

5 ROYALTY INCOME TRUSTS 42

- 5.1 Introduction and definition 42
- 5.2 Other benefits of royalty income trusts 43
- 5.3 Probable risks of royalty income trusts 43

6 OTHER TERMINOLOGIES ASSOCIATED WITH ROYALTY PAYMENTS 45

- 6.1 Lease Premium 45
- 6.2 Sub Lease 45
- 6.3 Royalty account 45
- 6.4 Royalty check 46
- 6.5 Tenet 46
- 6.6 Minimum Rent 46

6.7	Ground Rent	47
6.8	Shortworkings	47
6.9	Right of Recouping	47

7 SETTING ROYALTY RATES — 48

7.1	Introduction	48
7.2	How to set royalty rates in the fashion industry	48
7.3	How artist royalties are calculated	50
	7.3.1 Introduction	50
	7.3.2 Mechanical royalties	50
	7.3.3 Performance royalties	52
	7.3.4 The flow of money in the music industry	53
	7.3.5 How producers are paid	54
	7.3.6 The percentage received by artists' managers	55
7.4	How to calculate royalty rates for artworks	55
	7.4.1 General	55
	7.4.2 Deductions	56
	7.4.3 Per unit royalty negotiation	57
	7.4.4 One-time payment	58
	7.4.5 Gross and net sales	58
	7.4.6 Guaranteed Minimum Annual Royalty (GMAR) payment	58
	7.4.7 Auditing royalty income	59
	7.4.8 Upfront payment	60

8 PRACTICAL EXAMPLES FOR GENERATING ROYALTY INCOME — 61

8.1	Easiest way: Buy royalty income	61
	8.1.1 Royalty stocks or trusts	61
	8.1.2 Royalty Exchange	62
8.2	Generating royalty income as an author	64
	8.2.1 Introduction	64

8.2.2	Publishing via an agent	64
8.2.3	Self-publishing direct distribution	64
8.2.4	Getting started to self-publish on Amazon	65
8.2.5	Tips for success as an author	69
8.2.6	A few words on the ISBN	70

8.3 How to make revenue as a software developer 71

8.3.1	Introduction	71
8.3.2	Affiliate commissions	72
8.3.3	E-commerce	72
8.3.4	Subscription service	72

8.4 Making money from app development 72

8.5 How to make money from photo licensing 77

8.5.1	Introduction	77
8.5.2	Licensing options for photos	78
8.5.3	How to sell image licenses	79
8.5.4	Stock photography websites	79
8.5.5	Your website	81
8.5.6	Publications and magazines	82
8.5.7	Tips to help you when submitting your photos	82
8.5.8	Other Opportunity: Sell your prints	82
8.5.9	Other Opportunity: Start a niche photography business	83

8.6 How to get paid as an actor for TV shows 85

8.6.1	Overview	85
8.6.2	Payment on contracts	86
8.6.3	Earning more money as an actor	87
8.6.4	How to become a print model	90
8.6.5	Tips to becoming a successful commercial actor	91

8.7 Generating revenue as a fashion designer 92

9.1 Bonus: How to make money on YouTube 93

9.1.1	Creating a YouTube channel	93
9.1.2	Making money from YouTube music upload	95
9.1.3	Selling products or merchandise	96

    9.1.4   Working as an influencer or affiliate 97
    9.1.5   Licensing your contents (videos, news, etc.) to the media 98

10   MISCONCEPTIONS ABOUT ROYALTIES 99

10.1 Myths and misconceptions 99

10.2 Misconceptions in the music industry......................................99

10.3 Misconceptions about stock photo royalties..........................101

10.4 Misconceptions about book publishing royalties 101

10.5 Misconceptions about oil and gas royalties 102

10.6 Misconceptions about patents..103

10.7 Misconceptions about licensing 105

10.8 Misconceptions about copyright...107

1 Introduction

1.1 Overview

Intellectual property such as academic writings or discoveries, inventions, works of literary and artistic values, etc. need protection, especially if the goal of the protection is for economic value. Otherwise, they would be reproduced and redistributed without compensating the creator or owner. This puts the original creators and inventors at a great disadvantage. They lose a considerable amount of money. This is because of the costs involved in the production of the work or invention of the process as well as the risks involved during the process. For instance, research and development in the medical or space industry may cost a researching company billions of dollars.

In exchange for permission to use the copyrighted, licensed, or patented property, the owner receives a royalty payment. The owner retains ownership but only gives permission to the third party to manufacture, sell, or distribute the property for a fee. The company issuing the royalty can make royalty payments annually, daily, or as the case may be. The process of licensing involves two parties: the one that grants the license (otherwise known as 'the licensor') and the one that receives the license (otherwise known as 'the licensee').

Royalty payments are negotiable, redeemable, and convertible. They usually begin immediately upon the receipt of an investment. Therefore, it is necessary to research standards for royalty payments in the chosen industry as it will help to negotiate royalties appropriately and not deal on any unfair terms with the other party. If royalty payment is made to another party by you for using their work, such a payment constitutes a part of your business expenses.

Licensor gets its benefits by a licensee utilizing their intellectual property while the licensee receives greater benefits than the former receives. The goal of any licensee is profitability. They measure the amount of work to be done against the expected profit. Excessively high royalties will dissuade a licensee from working with the licensor. Generally, a licensing agreement that requires the licensee to pay more than 25% of its profits to the licensor may not have a sealed agreement as this is unfavorable to the licensee market.

1.2 Why are royalty payments important?

Below are some of the advantages of royalty payments:

- Unlike shares, royalties are a safer and more predictable investment. This is because of their easy and straightforward calculation.
- Accredited investors don't have to be registered securities before having permission to purchase and sell royalty contracts.
- Inflation does not affect royalty rates negatively. This is because royalties are only focused on revenues, which tend to increase during inflationary periods.
- Royalty payments are not fixed and increase with the rise in revenues of the issuing company.
- Even with the rise of issuer revenues and royalty payments increase, a purchaser can still sell royalties and make significant economic gains.
- Royalties are independent of revenue, and as such, losses made by a company have no effect on royalty payments.
- Revenue royalties can be collected as the royalty issuer earns revenue. A trustee-like service provider can gather royalties on a separate account on behalf of the investors.
- Royalties are not expected to be vulnerable to lower or discretionary payment from the issuing company.

- Personal agreements are not usually necessary while making or signing royalty contracts.
- If the finances earned for business development are utilized, the income tax deductibility of royalty investment is to the issuing company. However, the reverse might be the case if the amount received as royalty payment equals the initial royalty cost.

This book is a comprehensive guide to what the constituents of royalty payments are and to the reasons they are paid, the mode of calculating the rates, and how various industries and firms charge the payment. It also explains the step-by-step process of negotiating an arm's length terms of an agreement in royalty contracts. Any firm or intellectual property owner who wishes to negotiate appropriate royalty payments need to arm themselves with the information provided in this book. The book also covers royalty payments made in the following industries, with their respective applications: oil and gas, movie, art, photography, music, software, fashion, media, and book publishing. Each of the industries has been explained in a language that even a layman will understand.

2 What are Royalties?

2.1 Definition

Royalties are legally-binding payments made by one party to another party, usually an owner of a particular asset or property, for use of that property on an ongoing basis or over a specified period of time. The party that makes the payment is the licensee or franchisee while the owner of the property or asset is known as the licensor or franchisor. What constitutes a royalty payment is a valuable right usage.

The terms under which such property is licensed by one party to another is known as a license agreement. The license agreement spells out the type of asset, the geographic limitations of the royalties, the duration of the agreement, the royalty cuts (that is, percentage to be paid), etc. Where a government owns the resource, such license agreements can be regulated. Otherwise, they can follow a general structure for private contracts.

Usually, the assets classified under royalty payments may include, among others, patents, copyrights, trademarks, and franchises. They serve as a form of compensation to owners of such property. The amount to be paid is often agreed on a mutual ground – based on a certain percentage of the net revenues obtained from the use of the owner's property or other compensation metrics.

For instance, Microsoft Corporation is often paid royalties (percentage unknown) by computer manufacturers (such as IBM, HP, Dell, Compaq, etc.) for the right to use Microsoft's Windows operating system on their manufactured computers. Even popular fashion designers can charge royalties when other companies use their brand names and designs.

Both the royalty licensor (the person getting the payment) and the royalty licensee (the person making the payment) benefit from royalty agreements. While it helps the former to have access to a new market or increase an existing market share, the latter gets the opportunity to access products to which they could not have otherwise had access - this could be because of high production cost or the protection by patents.

2.2 Types of Royalty Agreements

Generally, royalty agreements are of two types: fixed price-per-unit and percentage-based agreements. The fixed price-per-unit agreement requires the licensor to be paid a set price on each unit of products the licensee sells. This type of agreement is often used in the case where the product of the licensor is a microcosm of a larger product the licensee produces. It also allows for the amount per unit to be adjusted in an inflationary situation.

An instance is a situation where Company A develops a RAM and gets it patented by the necessary authority. Company A then decides to seal a royalty agreement with ABC Computers to license the memory so that all computers manufactured by ABS Computers can include the memory as their components. In return, ABC Computers agrees to pay Company A the sum of $5 per every unit of memory it purchases. The cost of materials and labor for producing the memory is included in the price.

The second type is a percentage-based royalty. It requires the payment of a certain portion of revenues or operating profit realized from the sale of the product that was licensed. This is often used for standalone products or when the cost of the item usage is definite. An agreement based on the percentage of revenues is not as intricate as that involving operating profit.

Nevertheless, it is necessary to ensure that the percentage agreement is fair to both parties.

They need to agree on

- the actual product or property to be licensed (its uniqueness and market viability);
- the geographic limitation of the agreement;
- the length of the agreement;
- amount of the royalty to be paid;
- time and mode of payment (whether there would be an advance payment or not);
- record-keeping mode, and
- the propensity of the two parties to live up to the provisions of the agreement.

There should also be an explicit description of the property together with the provision of the name of the existing owner.

Irrespective of the type of agreement, it should contain the duration and the terms and conditions under which termination can occur or the basis for renewing the agreement. This is to avoid likely future controversies.

Other forms of royalty agreements include alliances (joint-ventures, franchises, and strategic alliances) and partnerships.

3 Different Industries that pay royalties

3.1 Music Industry

In the music industry, royalties are paid to musicians, songwriters, and writers of musical plays whenever commercial benefits are derived from their originally-recorded songs. This could be when they are played on the radio, used in movies or television, performed at bars, restaurants, and concerts, streamed, simulcast, webcast, or downloaded. The last four processes are made possible with the advent of the internet.

A musical composition cannot be protected from infringed use if it is not yet registered with a copyright authority or agency. Recording companies and the performing artists often enjoy a distinct set of copyrights and royalties privileges when a third party: records the composed music on CDs and tapes, performs the song on stage or television and uses the song as an adaptation in movies, television advertisements, etc.

Producers receive royalty payments based on the recordings they are able to complete, and the copies of audio products (that is, CD) sold in the market. The latter is known as record loyalty. It provides an easy avenue to earn extra money based on audio product demand and publicity. However, this requires the clearance of rights and royalty management licenses.

3.2 Oil and gas Industry

Also in the oil and gas industry, landowners are paid a royalty rate by companies for the right to extract certain natural resources from the landed property of the owner. Such resources, among others, include natural gas and petroleum. Such a royalty payment is based on percentage agreement of the lease, excluding production costs the lessee expended.

The value of oil royalties may also be exchanged in oil. The lessor receives it and markets it on behalf of the lessee. However, receiving cash payment royalty seems preferable as receiving it in oil may put the landowner at a disadvantage - especially if they are not knowledgeable enough.

In the same vein, royalty payments are also received in monetary terms in exchange for gas. This is because the prices of gas are difficult to value as the market is volatile and keeps fluctuating. Clauses of contracts of a gas royalty usually state a royalty payment as proceeds. However, this could be in market value or in kind. A royalty clause specifies the amount to be paid to the Lessor, the deadline for receipt of the payments, interest rates for late payments, and other terms and conditions.

The mining industry also has similar agreements in existence, as minerals such as copper and silver could be mined based on royalty agreement.

3.3 Patents

Patents are intangible assets that provide the owner of such assets an exclusive right to prevent others from practicing such a patented technology in the country where the patent was issued. The patent could be given for a period of 20 years. A patent license requires that the patent owner is paid royalties in exchange for the right to practice any of the basic patent rights including manufacturing, usage, sale, or importing.

Patent rights may be licensed out either on an exclusive or non-exclusive basis. They may be subject to time or territorial limitations. They may also cover a whole technology or an aspect of technology.

There are three varieties of patents, vis-à-vis: design, plant, and utility patents. Design patent provides an exclusive right to the creator of a new, unique ornamental design for a product. An instance is the making of a new beverage bottle design. Rather than protect its structure, a design patent covers only an appearance.

Plant patents are issued to botanists who have grafted and created asexually propagated plants (such as new hybrid plants, cultivated sports, and mutants) which are also capable of reproduction. Such plants are reproduced by means such as budding, layering, grafting, and inarching. Utility patents are granted to inventors and discoverers of any new and useful improvement such as a machine, process, article of manufacture, or matter composition (U.S. Patent and Trademark Office).

Patents serve as an incentive avenue and invention security for individuals or companies who are involved in the development of new products or services to continue with the process, while also ruling out the possibility of infringement by other parties. For instance, large pharmaceutical companies often spend as huge as billions of dollars on research and development. In the absence of patents, companies without capital investment in research and development can easily duplicate as well as distribute or sell their drugs and medicines. In other words, patents protect the profitability tendencies of companies with intellectual property.

Applying for a patent often requires the inventor or discoverer to provide technical information about the invention to the public. A market feasibility study including costs of start-up, market demand, the safety of the invention, and production feasibility to determine the marketability of the new idea has to be carried out.

It also requires the company to conduct in-depth research to see if a patent for a similar invention has been claimed by another entity, which may be an individual or an institution. There are also some fees associated with it, with a confirmation of the authenticity of the invention - which could also be a modification or an improvement of an existing invention.

Usually, the patent process may take from one year to several years. If a patent is discovered to be too close to another, application for such a patent can be rejected.

Instances of patents

In 1904, King C. Gillette patented the razor, which was later dubbed a "safety razor."

In 1923, Garrett Morgan received a patent for the traffic light invention.

Philo Taylor Farnsworth invented the first television system in 1930 and was issued a patent.

3.4 Art

Artists don't need to continue reproducing new original works to have a stream of income. Licensing an artwork has a significant economic benefit, particularly in terms of receiving a royalty from individuals or firms when they reproduce the artistic work. Despite giving out the license, such artists still retain the original ownership (that is, copyright or design patent) of the work.

For instance, an artist may create an image - probably a cat painting, while an entity (such as a manufacturing store) seeks their permission to use the image on T-shirts, which will be sold. The artist grants the company permission in exchange for a royalty payment. In other words, the company takes responsibility for the production and sales of the T-shirt while the artist gets a certain percentage of the gross revenue, based on agreed terms of the license. Such a licensed property could also be offered for other purposes.

Art (Resale) Royalty is a royalty payment made upon the resale of artworks such as sculptures, ceramics, engravings, graphic works (collage, drawing, painting, etc.), glassware, lithograph, photographs, tapestry, etc. The owner of artwork can only receive a royalty payment if the copy of the work is only one of a limited number the artist made. Nevertheless, the net economic benefits of art resale royalties to artists remain highly contested.

3.5 Photos

Stock photography agencies employ a royalty license to sell stock images. This license grants the buyer – other than the owner – the right to use the image in various ways, for either a one-time or flat fee. The proceeds from the sale of a license are split between the photographer and the agency. Some licenses require the customer to pay certain royalties to the agency, the copyright owner, or even both, every time they use the photo. Stock agencies only sell to buyers the right to use the photos; they don't transfer the ownership of the photos. The photographer or photo creator still remains the owner of the photo or image while also having the permission to sell their works as many times as they wish. This creates for them a legal stream of income.

3.6 Trademarks

Trademarks are distinctive expressions or features used by brands to distinguish themselves from other brands. These expressions may include slogans, words, logos, and sounds. It aims at assuring the public of the quality of products or services offered by a particular brand. With it, consumers, in turn, develop a high sense of security, belonging, and value appeals to the brand.

A trademark right is offered to a third party to sell goods or market services under a mark, with an exclusive right, within a particular geographical location. It is often applied to an entire brand. This means that any product - not just one - produced by the brand has the trademark.

Companies seek to license another owner's trademark to achieve brand recognition rather than taking the risk and paying the heavy cost implication of entering the market with its yet-to-be-recognized brand name. However, this comes with the assurance that the quality of the goods will meet the required standards.

The expression of percentages of trademark royalties is similar to those of patents. When negotiating rates, companies often assess the profit prospects they will likely make if sales and prices increase.

3.7 Software

Software is often categorized under literary, artistic or scientific work. Though there seem to be some disparities about its right classification, however, the fact remains that it could be copyrighted. Software royalty agreements are for the license of existing marketable software technology. In other words, software royalty is obtained when the software is purchased for reproduction and either on-license or on-sale. Software royalty rates are considered in relation to its total development cost, break-even cost, risk in development, and whether or not it requires maintenance.

The following types of software payments exist:

- transfer of copyright rights for commercial exploitation
- transfer of a copy of the computer program
- site/enterprise/network license arrangements (permission to use the program on a single site or a network)
- supply of information
- transfer of software ownership
- development services (where a customer gets a software development company to develop new software or modify existing software on their behalf, while also transferring the right to use, sell, or distribute such software.

Most software has the agreement terms to the sale of all rights to use the program under a license.

3.8 Fashion

The industry is an Intellectual Property intensive one. In the fashion industry, designers can license the right to use their brand names on items of clothing by other industries in exchange for royalties. The established brand or designer provides other firms with its trademarks to manufacture and distribute other types of products. The ultimate goal is for the consumers to perceive the brand as an entity, with no variation in quality.

Brands such as Ralph Lauren and Calvin Klein have sold royalties to new companies. For instance, the Hermès Kelly bag and the Stella McCartney collection are creative works that bear the Nike logo. These brands have used a distinctive brand – probably someone's intellectual effort in a bid to attract goodwill through its use. In other words, some popular have allowed other brands to use their brand names to grow their brand awareness and image building at certain royalty rates. Royalty rates in the fashion industry are based on a percentage of sales usually between five percent and 15 percent - of the licensed goods.

There are measures that have been put to place to ensure the full enforcement of and compliance with the rights associated with intellectual property. This is to deter counterfeiters and copycats who, rather than investing the needed capital and time in initiating new ideas and creating innovative works, prefer copying already-existing fashion designs. This is because it is very difficult to protect a brand, image, and designs in the fashion industry from being counterfeited. However, consumers belonging to the elite class, especially, attach considerable status benefits to the purchase of the "real" fashion item from the original brand.

It is vital to define the agreement terms within a limited scope. This is to ensure the maintenance of control over other prospective licensing opportunities when the need to include other partners arises. In other words, licensing rights should be as narrowly as possible. For instance, it should cover the particular products to be included, the type of distribution (domestic, international, or both), the platform for selling (online, offline, or both), agreement type and the option for renewal or termination, and maintenance of quality control.

3.9 Book publishing

In book publishing, authors and writers often receive a certain percentage of the sales price (as royalties) in exchange for the exclusive use of their books by other industries. These payments are often made by publishers who print in book formats. In the United States, for instance, every published book, newspaper, or magazine is protected by copyright. This implies that anyone - other than the publisher - who wishes to reproduce any portion of the print product must make a royalty payment each time of use.

Royalty payments in the publishing industry are of two types: net-sales and retail-price royalties. Net-sales royalty payments are made when authors receive certain from the publisher after the total discounts given to retail stores have been subtracted from the net income. In other words, publishers pay a percentage of the amount they receive after printing, distribution, and retail discounts have been subtracted. Publishers often sell books to bookstores on discounts since they buy in large quantities. Average royalties paid on net sales range between 16% and 26%, for hardcover and trade paperback.

Royalties paid on retail price, also known as list royalties, are the percentage paid to the author by the publisher on each unit of the book sold. Generally, the average retail royalties range falls between 10% and 15% on sales of Hardcover, and 5% and 7.5% on sales of Trade Paperback.

For instance, if a book sells for $20 and the royalty percentage (of the retail price), based on an undersigned agreement, is 10, then the publisher pays the author $2 on every unit of the book sold. In other words, if the publisher sells 10,000 copies of the book, it implies that the author's royalty will amount to $20,000. However, if the publisher has paid an advance of $10,000 to the author before the sealing of the royalty agreement, the latter only gets $10,000 to balance the expected royalty amount of $20,000.

3.10 Television

Also, satellite TV services often pay some network stations a certain rate as royalty to broadcast certain channels over their stations. The calculation for cable residuals depends on the channel and frequency or type of use. Notwithstanding, actors and playwrights receive a considerable amount of residual checks each time their works are reused.

When a streaming service purchases a show, or syndicates or redistributes it, the actors received royalty payments. Shows such as Friends, Seinfeld, Gilligan's Island, Everybody Loves Raymond, to mention but a few, continue to yield residual checks worth millions of dollars to the principal performers.

4 Royalty agreement tips for licensees and licensors

4.1 General

For licensees

- The licensor should have stable finances and be able to adapt to changing technological innovations and industrial shifts.
- The licensor should also have a clear plan highlighting the product goals, research and development plans, and new or related product development prospects.
- The licensor should be able to provide adequate customer service and support levels to both the licensee and the consumers - an essential requirement for high-tech or complex products.

For licensors

- The licensee should have a strong history of financial viability, wide territorial coverage, market credibility, and a high rate of product sale.
- The licensee should also show signs of future growth and original product maintenance prospects.

Irrespective of the agreement terms, the rates should be gauged correctly to ensure that the buyer and the seller are willing, and the transaction occurs at arms-length rather than under compulsion.

4.2 Royalty contracts

Royalty contracts are usually established agreements to accommodate the needs and interests of the parties involved in the exchange of intellectual property rights for a royalty payment. The payments are made as a percentage of the net or total revenues earned from the use of intellectual property.

The contract or agreement states, among others, the responsibilities of the party (that receives the right) on keeping of records, the heir to whom the royalty payments would be transferred if the property owner dies, and the standards for terminating the agreement.

4.3 Conditions for terminating a royalty agreement

One mistake parties in a royalty agreement tend to make is not having clear-cut terms and conditions of agreement termination. As much as the interests of the involving parties should be duly represented and explicitly captured in the agreement, there may be a breach of contract along the line.

For instance, a licensee may challenge a patent, go bankrupt, or undergo a change of control. These could result in the consideration of the option of terminating the contract by the affected party. There are some instances where the damaged party seeks damages.

Terminating a royal agreement has a significant legal and business implication. Thus, great caution must be taken to avoid being enmeshed in a legal entanglement that will impact the financial state of the firm negatively.

4.4 A case of an agreement termination

4.4.1 General

An inventor made the decision to sell his line of varying sizes of plastic products to a large plastic company. He seeks to receive royalty payments on every unit of the plastic products sold. The royalty agreement was supposed to last for a period of ten years. The royalty rates for the varying categories of plastic products differ, and fall under two categories: the original product as commercialized by the inventor and the byproducts derived from the original product.

Based on the agreement and rates, the company paid the inventor royalties on the product sale. However, the inventor accused the company of its deliberate action of wrongly classifying the plastic products to evade the payment of royalties.

4.4.2 Options available

The inventor was faced with the options of either suing for the previous due underpayments, or terminating the agreement completely and seek damages based on the royalty agreement terms. Choosing the first option might jeopardize his future dealings with the company. The company might initiate some means of depriving him of his benefits (that is, royalties) in the future.

However, the second option implies that he could terminate the agreement as well as sue the company for the recovery of the total royalty earnings accruable to him by rights if the terms of the agreement had not been breached.

4.4.3 Justifying the termination

The party terminating the agreement must prove that the 'breach' (as done by the other party) is essential to the terms and purpose of the contract. The court would then have to decide if the breach was significant and justifiable for the proposed agreement termination. If proven to be true, the court then makes its judgment based on some legalities. To avoid a complete termination based on a trivial breach or giving an unfair advantage to any party, the court will consider many factors, such as the effect of the breach on the benefits accruable to the terminating party, the extent of forfeiture the breaching party will suffer, and the likelihood of the breaching party to pay for their breach.

4.4.4 Comparison

The case exemplified above indicates the underpayment of royalties against the withholding of royalties. There are varying state laws on the conditions for terminating a royalty agreement contract. Thus, there is no general rule. In some states, a minor breach is enough for termination, while in others, it is not enough ground for termination. However, the definition of "minor" becomes relative and specific to state laws.

4.4.5 Consequences of the wrong termination

The terminating party, despite its claim of underpayment of royalties, may turn out to create significant damages and expenses for itself. For instance, the licensee may pull products off shelves or countersue the terminating party for improper termination of the contract.

4.4.6 Solution

To avoid the uncertainty and controversies that usually surround the grounds for terminating a royalty contract, it is vital to specify the standards for contract termination based on what both parties consider important to them. In other words, the termination clause should be specific in highlighting conduct or events that can necessitate a termination. These might include royalties underpayment, noncompliance with an audit, or specific misuses of intellectual property (to be clearly stated).

Also, the provisions should include the fate of the intellectual property upon contract termination. Does the licensee retain ownership of the IP? Or it gets reverted to the licensor? Thus, every termination must comply with the termination provisions or standards of the contract.

4.5 Royalty Income

Royalty income is simply the income derived from allowing someone to use intellectual property such as artistic or literary works, etc. and exploit natural resources such as minerals, etc. The payments also include the use of trademarks and patents. Royalties are legally binding. Many times, the individual utilizing the property does so for income generation.

Generally, royalty income is of two kinds: copyrights, trademarks, and patent royalties, and oil, gas, or minerals extraction royalties. For instance, Microsoft, a hi-tech software giant, earned billions of dollars from computer manufacturers, such as Compaq, Dell, Hewlett-Packard (HP), etc. Smartphone manufacturers such as Nokia and

Samsung are not ruled out in the purchase of Microsoft's intellectual property. These manufacturers use software products invented by Microsoft, especially the Windows operating system. In 2013, Microsoft received $1 billion as a royalty payment from Samsung.

5 Royalty income trusts

5.1 Introduction and definition

A royalty income trust, also known as an investment trust, is a financing option with the aim of retaining investments or cash flows in an operating company. It is distinct from a stock or bond, though it also has a separate legal entity. The San Juan Basin Royalty Trust (SJT), one of the largest royalty trusts in the United States, owns the Burlington Resources royalties. The latter is a company that deals with oil exploration and production.

For instance, XYZ Oil Company wants to sell its maturing oil wells with significant rates of production and reserves, and with a million barrels of annual production. If each unit of barrels sells for $10, it means the annual income amounts to $10 million. If XYZ Oil Company accepts the suggestion of an investment bank that it should consider a royalty trust, it is to the former's advantage. It implies that the investment company makes a payout payment to XYZ Oil Company, while still managing the company for a fee.

Investors often see great prospects in royalty trusts as they promise higher yields than stocks and bonds. Companies intending to sell assets that produce cash flow also find royalty trusts as attractive.

Generally, royalty income trusts purchase the rights to earn royalty payments on the production and sale of companies with natural resources. The profits realized from the sale then go to the owners of the trust unit.

5.2 Other benefits of royalty income trusts

The fact that royalty income trusts are attractive to investors and companies is an indication that they place those entities on great tax advantages. This is because an operating company has its natural resources depreciating and depleted over time. Also, rather than the IRS to consider distributions from royalty income trusts income, they can be used by investors to minimize their stock cost basis. When the stock gets liquidated, the IRS only continues taxing after the owner might have sold their shares. However, they take the proceeds from capital gains, though at a lower or reduced rate.

Royalty income trusts are not double-taxed as they are transiting investment vehicles. Those who hold royalty trust units are qualified for certain tax credits when they produce fuels from sources other than the conventional ones.

5.3 Probable risks of royalty income trusts

Royalty income trusts cash flows are volatile both in prices of commodities and levels of production. The fact that they do not provide steady cash flows (like MLPs) makes it a risky venture for investors. Usually, trusts lack independent management, employees, operations, etc., making investors have less control and vulnerable to being removed from their output.

6 Other terminologies associated with royalty payments

6.1 Lease Premium

This is an additional payment made by a lessee to a lessor. Note that this differs from the royalty payment already established in the royalty agreement. It is often treated as a capital expenditure. This implies that it is written off every year through profit and loss account. This is also done using the most suitable method.

6.2 Sub Lease

This involves the subletting some part of a land or mine by the landlord. The beneficiary of such a sublet is known as a sub-lessee whose lessee becomes their lessor. The lessee still maintains their position with the landlord.

6.3 Royalty account

When royalty agreements are made, there is usually an account where the lessor receives the royalty payment for intellectual property (that is, patent, copyright, etc.). This account is known as a royalty account. It is used for the collection of payments on a regular basis, which may run into a financial year.

With a royalty account, the two parties have access to a good record of all transactions and particulars. The balance is easily transferrable to a Profit & Loss account for appropriate evaluation.

6.4 Royalty check

A royalty check is a reward earned from the sale of creative work. For instance, for a writer, the amount earned from the sale of each copy of the book is a royalty check. A song composer gets their royalty check when someone - other than the original creator - performs the song professionally or buys a copy of the CD. Land or property owners also earn royalty check when another party purchases their mineral rights, that is, on oil and gas. The period of earning a royalty check depends on the royalty agreement. It could be annually, half-yearly or quarterly.

6.5 Tenet

This refers to a publisher or an author. It could also be used to describe a lessee or patentor who takes out personal or commercial rights from the owner on lease.

6.6 Minimum Rent

This is a popular term in the lease agreement. It is used to describe a guarantee (in terms of minimum, fixed, or dead rent) a lessee makes to a lessor for likely output, production, or sale shortage. The implication is that the lessor gets a minimum fix rent independent of the circumstances surrounding probable shortage.

6.7 Ground Rent

Also known as surface rent, it is the rent a landlord receives for the use of their land for a particular period, usually on a yearly or half-yearly basis.

6.8 Shortworkings

Shortworkings are the difference between the minimum rent and the actual royalty. In other words, the basis for paying royalty is minimum rent, which results from production or sale shortage.

6.9 Right of Recouping

If a royalty agreement provides the option of recovering minimum rent excess over the actual royalty, it is known as the right of recoupment (of the excess, that is, shortworkings). It is usually for a fixed or floating period. It is fixed if it gets into force from the point of making the royalty agreement. If it does not take effect from the point of making the royalty agreement, the right of recouping could be said to be floating.

7 Setting royalty rates

7.1 Introduction

The idea of setting royalty rates is peculiar to every industry - whether fashion, oil and gas, music, movie, or publishing. Basically, intellectual property usually licensed includes copyrights, trademarks, and patents. Trade secrets, brands, designs, etc. could be licensed as well.

When setting royalty rates, it is important to consider the specifics of the industry. This is to ensure a favorable or fair royalty rate is set.

7.2 How to set royalty rates in the fashion industry

Setting fashion royalty rates

Setting fashion royalty rates depend on the intellectual property being licensed. It is recommended to get comparable royalty rates for pricing transfer. Comparable rates are a good reflection of market rates. The following stems will help in setting a royalty rate that is at arm's length.

Select an appropriate royalty structure

Royalty rates in the fashion industry can be fixed or floating. A fixed structure implies that the same amount would be received for the use of intellectual property, irrespective of the total sales or profits made by the licensee. The floating structure is built on a certain percentage of the gross or net revenue generated by the use or distribution of the intellectual property. This is based on the property's current value and profitability.

Calculate a fair royalty percentage

This requires market-based (that is, setting royalty rates by comparing license agreements) or income-based (setting royalty rates based on the expected revenue of the intellectual property) approaches. Examples of the market-based approach include the comparable uncontrolled transaction (CUT) and comparable uncontrolled price (CUP) method. Income-based approaches include residual income and profit split methods.

Irrespective of the approach to employ, it is essential to have access to current, reliable data for comparison. This will help to ensure that the rates are reasonable. To use the income-based approach, it is important to work out the earning potentials of intellectual property. If the property licensed is to be sold alone, the process of calculating the rate follows the usual pattern. However, if it involves another intellectual property, the proportion of the revenue attributable to it needs to be calculated.

7.3 How artist royalties are calculated

7.3.1 Introduction

Music royalties for performing and recording artists are calculated based on a percentage of total record sales of the composition. They also take into consideration the artist's fan base and the earning potentials of the music composition. They are calculated using the following criteria:

7.3.2 Mechanical royalties

Mechanical royalties vary according to rate from countries to countries. For instance, in the United States, the rate is $0.091 per digital download and CD. This implies that the owner of the composition gets 9.1 cents each time the recording is dubbed into a CD or downloaded online.

Royalties from physical CDs are calculated thus: the number of sales multiplied by wholesale price multiplied by royalty rate. In other words, if the wholesale price of an album $20 and the royalty rate is 10%, the owner earns $2. The record label gets the remaining $18.

As already discussed, the royalty rate to be given to artists depends on the fan base. For instance, while superstar artists may command about 18-20%, and mid-range artists get 15-18%, new artists may get only 13-16%.

With the evolution of technology, streaming tends to be the dominant means of consuming music. This leads artists receiving a royalty on each music stream. The rate of streaming royalty is not fixed and not on a "per play" basis. Songwriters only receive a meager 15% of the total revenues earned when their songs are streamed by users. This is quite less than royalties earned on master recordings. This shows a large earning gap between the streaming platform and the artist or songwriter or music composer.

For instance, despite the claims by Spotify that it pays a fair percentage per stream to artists who have their songs uploaded on its platform, numerous artists often complain of low share. Spotify, a top streaming platform, has about 75 million users and made about $6 billion in 2018. Streaming services only benefit chart-topping artists such as Drake and Cardi B. Other streaming services include Apple Music, Deezer, and YouTube Music. Unless there are new royalties negotiations, streaming royalties will continue to favor big artists greatly while new or small ones won't earn a substantial living wage.

7.3.3 Performance royalties

Performance royalties are generated from recording, public performance, playing, and streaming of copyrighted works. Public spaces include restaurants / bars / clubs, radio, television, live concerts, etc. They also include music streaming services. Performance royalties are negotiated between the streaming service and the affiliated PROs (Performing Rights Organizations) privately. PROs collect performance royalties on behalf of artists. The three major PROs in the United States are BMI, ASCAP, and SESAC. To start earning songwriter and publishing royalties, it is necessary to affiliate and register the songs with a PRO.

Performance royalties are split into two equal halves with songwriter royalties taking one half and publishing royalties constituting the other half. Songwriter royalties are paid out to the original owners of the composition. For publishing royalties, publishing can be outsourced to a third-party publishing company. In order not to miss out on the 50% associated with publishing royalties, it is essential to sign to a Publishing Administration Company. The Company receives publishing royalties on behalf of the song owner.

7.3.4 The flow of money in the music industry

The flow of money depends on the status of the artist and the label to which they are signed. Labels include major record labels, independent labels, or an independent musician.

When an artist is signed to a major record label, the money received for sound recording copyright is paid directly to the record label while the percentage to be earned by the artist depends on the record contract. This may range from 10 to 50%.

For new artists, a record label may take between 50-90% of the total earnings while the artist takes between 10-16%. This is because record labels take upon themselves all the financial risks involved in breaking and marketing a new artist. Also, it is not every artist that labels sign that yields a profit. Thus, they need to augment losses incurred on the failed acts with their successful acts.

The royalty rate for a session musician on a track or album is between 1-2%.

For independent labels, the Publishing Administration takes 15-20%, the publisher takes 50%, while the songwriter takes the remaining. For the sound recording, the aggregators, charged with the responsibility of the global distribution of music on digital stores and streaming platforms, also take a percentage of each sale. The cut the artist receives here is often greater than a major record label's.

The third category - independent musician - differs from an independent label as they face the task of getting their mechanical licensing agent (who collects mechanical streaming royalties) as well as a publishing administrator based on their clout as an artist. Publishing administrators such as Songtrust or Tunecore. Usually, the record label of an independent musician tends to take a significant cut of the total earnings, however, the benefit is that they get to keep all their cut all alone.

For sound recording, the job description of aggregators (as explained under the independent label) for independent musicians is a digital distribution only. The distributor makes the music available to music retailers and streaming sites. Just like the independent label, digital distributors collect a portion of every sale.

7.3.5 How producers are paid

Producers earned through a Work for Hire Agreement, advance fee, or points (also known as album points or producer royalties). A point is equal to 1% of the total revenue the song is able to make. In other words, 2% amounts to 2 points.

If the points are awarded on some songs on an album, rather than the entire album, the percentage is calculated differently. For instance, if the producer is awarded 2 points on 6 songs on a 12 songlist album, they receive 6/12 of 2 percent of the album's music royalties earnings, amounting to only 1%.

7.3.6 The percentage received by artists' managers

A manager is essential to an artist's career. They are a cheerleader and guide through every business decision of the artist. Their importance makes them entitled to up to 15-20% of the gross earnings of an artist. This implies a percentage of what the artist earns as against what they keep.

7.4 How to calculate royalty rates for artworks

7.4.1 General

It is vital to have proper knowledge of how to calculate royalty rates for artworks. This is partly to ensure that the licensee is paying the licensor appropriately. The rates for licensing artwork depend greatly on the artwork, its size, and the resources of the negotiating company.

The most convenient approach to contracts and license agreements between the licensor and the licensee is to agree on a royalty percentage. This method reflects the amount licensees pay in relation to their current business situation. Licensees pay less when the licensed artwork is not yet profitable and more when it starts generating increased revenues. Similarly, the licensor gets their percentage in proportion to the generated revenues.

To calculate royalty payments, the royalty rate is multiplied by net sales. In other words, the royalty rate x net sales. For instance, if a royalty rate is 10% and the net sales are $1,000. The net sales royalty will be 10% multiplied by $1,000. This equals to $100.

Some royalty estimates include the following:

- 2-5% for greeting cards and gift wrap
- 3-8% for household items such as cups, pots, sheets, towels, etc.
- 2-10% for fabrics, apparel (caps, shirts, T-shirts, caps, trousers, decals)
- Minimum of 10% for posters and prints
- 3-8% for toys and dolls

7.4.2 Deductions

These are items that are deducted from sales (of the artwork) before the calculation of the royalty. Generally, there is the conventional practice of the licensee deducting certain amounts (for taxes, returns, credits, shipping costs, and discounts) from gross sales. Deductions determine what a licensor receives at the end of the day. For instance, a licensor who receives a royalty rate of 2% of net or gross sales without deductions may earn beyond what they would ordinarily earn from, for instance, a 5% royalty rate that has deductions of various licensee expenses.

Most importantly, when entering a royalty agreement, a licensor should try as much as possible to avoid deductions for bad debts and uncollectible accounts, sales commission, vague fees, and marketing, promotion, or advertising costs. Rather than asking for individual deductions during negotiations, it is preferable for a licensor to set a specific percentage for deductions, which should be fixed. Fixed deductions imply that the portion remains unchanged throughout the period the licensing contract covers. Also, it implies that if the licensed artwork achieves quick and substantial growth and profit rates, the royalty payment is not increased proportionally.

7.4.3 Per unit royalty negotiation

Certain cases may warrant the need for artists to negotiate a "per unit royalty." This may be based on sold or manufactured units of artworks, rather than the total earnings received from the sales. For instance, for each of manufactured or sold (licensed) artwork, an artist can earn $.75 royalty.

7.4.4 One-time payment

A licensee may, based on negotiation, pay an artist a license fee once. This is usually done at the initial stage of the contract agreement. This fee differs from an advance fee payment, which is usually deductible from royalties.

7.4.5 Gross and net sales

Customers who purchase a licensed artwork are billed some amount. The total amount is known as gross sales. Net sales, on the other hand, are calculated by deducting certain deductions (cost of the artwork, shipment costs, etc.) from the revenue realized from the sale of the licensed product. This is done prior to the calculation and payment of the royalty.

7.4.6 Guaranteed Minimum Annual Royalty (GMAR) payment

As an artist, if you encounter a company that shows a great deal of interest in your artwork and would also prefer a long-term license, negotiating a GMAR payment might become necessary. It involves the payment of a certain amount, usually at the start of each year, by the licensee, irrespective of the depth of sales by the merchandise during the year.

If, at the end of the year, the royalties the artist earns exceed the GMAR, the difference is paid to them. Also, if the GMAR is more than the total royalties the artist earns (that is, the artist gets paid more than the earnings from the product), the licensee takes a loss. However, this may depend on whether or not the licensee and licensor had an initial agreement and negotiation to apply the difference to GMARs in subsequent years.

7.4.7 Auditing royalty income

Usually, licensees are expected to pay the appropriate royalty rates to artists. However, the artist might be unable to ascertain if the number of sold products as claimed by the licensee is the true reflection. To forestall the likelihood of a shortfall, it is necessary to make an audit provision in the agreement. The provision should:

- indicate the period when the artist or their representative (e.g., business manager or financial auditor) can have access to licensee records, and
- include the compensation to be made upon the discovery of an error of a certain sum and magnitude during the audit. The licensee will be required to compensate the artist for the shortfall, as well as cater for the costs of the audit.

Also, provisions should be made for attorney's fees for the probability of having to institute litigation for royalties or audit costs against the licensee. The fees cover the required legal fees.

7.4.8 Upfront payment

This is when an "advance" fee payment is made at the time of signing a license agreement. It could be "recouped" against royalties not yet made or received, unless if the agreement states otherwise. A licensee forecasts the possible royalties to be earned by a licensor and pays them. For instance, a licensee can expect a license owner to receive $2,000 as royalty. When the licensor starts earning royalties, the licensee keeps the first $2,000 to repay itself the advance. However, if the royalty earned by the artist falls below that, the licensee bears the loss. The licensor only returns the advance when it breaches the provision of the agreement. Thus, an upfront payment provides financial security for the licensor.

8 Practical examples for generating royalty income

8.1 Easiest way: Buy royalty income

8.1.1 Royalty stocks or trusts

At stock exchanges, there are shares available of certain companies that get nearly all their income from royalty payments.

Examples (these are not recommendations!):

Franco-Nevada Corporation (FNV.TO) – This is a Canadian company owning gold royalties and gold royalty streams. This is quite a special business model within "gold stock". However, it works fine.

The dividend yield was around 1 % (September 2019).

Freehold Royalties Ltd. (FRU.TO) – FRU is an oil and gas royalty company. The dividend yield was around 8 % (September 2019).

Alaris Royalty Corporation (AD.TO) – A Private Equity company that finances other companies in exchange for royalties or distributions from the Private Company Partners. The dividend yield was around 8% (September 2019) and dividends are paid monthly.

Pizza Pizza Royalty Corporation (PZA.TO) – This company gets its income from franchises (772 Pizza-Restaurants). The dividend yield was around 8 – 9 % (September 2019) and dividends are paid monthly.

Disclaimer: These are no recommendations. Please do your own research. Figures are not up-to-date, naturally.

These companies are just a few examples. There are many more. I especially recommend browsing dividend stocks of the Canadian Stock Exchanges. They very often offer monthly dividends.

8.1.2 Royalty Exchange

In addition, royalty income streams can be acquired on certain platforms. The largest and most professional one I know is Royalty Exchange for music royalties.

Royalty Exchange has always some offers on its website and works as an auction site. Royalty owners normally sell there their royalty interest for a duration of 10 years or for a lifetime. There are various kind of rights, whereof the royalty interest can be acquired. Starting prices vary very much, lower ones begin at about USD 4'000. The latest development is that they have opened a marketplace where you can buy or sell your bought royalty interests again. However, they take a commission for that.

My experiences show that Royalty Exchange is highly professional in doing its business. Every step is executed digitally; so no need to do paperwork at home. They guide you properly with e-mails through the whole process once you have won an auction. Royalty income comes with the promised periodicity. You get a very detailed royalty statement with every payment. Providing and archiving works through Paymenthub.com, digitally, as well.

8.2 Generating royalty income as an author

8.2.1 Introduction

Authors who seek to make royalties from their published books need to find a literary agent. Usually, agents do not charge them until their work is sold. However, they could be charged for ancillary expenses such as photocopying and postage.

8.2.2 Publishing via an agent

When an agent sells a licensed book on behalf of the author, they receive 15% and 20% of the proceeds for domestic rights and foreign rights, respectively. The 20% is split equally between the primary agent and the subagent.

Royalties in the publishing industry vary. For hardcover, trade paperback, books, and mass market paperback, the retail and net rates include 10-15%, 6-7.5%, 25%, and 8-10%, respectively. Others such as special sales and high discounts have varying definitions and splits.

8.2.3 Self-publishing direct distribution

Authors can also self-publish their books by visiting the platforms that are publishing their books directly. On every copy sold, they receive a certain percentage.

For publishing on Amazon Kindle Direct, a paperback attracts 60% of the proceeds while an ebook attracts 70%. However, if it exceeds $9.99, it only attracts 35%.

On Audible, an audiobook attracts 40% and 25% exclusive and nonexclusive payments for authors.

For Barnes & Noble Press, an author earns 55% on paperback (this excludes printing costs), 65% of proceeds on the book if priced above $2.99. If otherwise, it stands at 40%.

For Kobo platform, the author earns 70% on books priced at about $2.99.

8.2.4 Getting started to self-publish on Amazon

Amazon Kindle platform allows authors to publish both books and paperbacks. The steps involved in the process include the following:

1. Manuscript and cover preparation.

Prepare your manuscript and cover in compliance with Kindle content and quality guidelines. You find all the necessary information about formatting on the amazon website. Amazon offers a help tool to create your cover and also provides you with very detailed layout instructions for your book texts.

2. Create an Amazon account to sign in to KDP (Kindle Direct Publishing)

To set up an Amazon account,

- Visit https://kdp.amazon.com and follow the instructions.
- The next step is to click Update in the account information section and fill in tax information. It's compulsory to complete this section BEFORE you can publish your first book.
- Upon completion, click "Finish". This returns you to the main page and your profile is complete.

Note that banking information may be requested as Amazon will wire royalties to the account on some bases.

3. Select a book title and subtitle

This section is one of the determiners of the fan base your book will attract. Though a subtitle is optional, it is necessary to provide some tags to your book in this section. It brings views and creates stronger intrigue. It also helps people easily locate your book when searching. Make sure to keep it unique, concise, and clear.

4. Write a description for your book

Your book requires a powerful book description for potential buyers to have a clue of what your book is all about. Though a bit of it is already covered under the cover and subtitle section, they want more detailed information. Amazon does not require an ISBN code.

5. Select the appropriate Amazon category

Amazon provides a wide range of categories and subcategories collections from which to select. The goal is to look for less competitive but trending areas. You can check Amazon rankings for a clue of less competitive categories

6. Upload manuscript to Amazon

This is where you upload your book to the platform. You must first save your manuscript in a supported kindle format.

- Visit the "Your Bookshelf" page in your KDP account.
- Locate and select "Kindle book Actions". It is close to the book title section.
- Select Edit book Content.
- Select "Upload book manuscript".
- Locate and select the manuscript on your computer and click on "Upload".
- Upload complete!

Once Amazon finishes with the file upload, you will receive a confirmation message where you can preview the uploaded file to check for likely errors. It allows for multiple uploads as the new version uploaded can easily override the existing one. Also, at this stage, you can have an overview of how the inside of your book looks like, using the "Look Inside" feature.

7. Create a book cover

A perfect book cover design is necessary to publish a successful book on Amazon. It is no longer news that a book cover design that looks attractive will compel prospective buyers to check out the book. Examples of freelancing sites include 99 Designs, 100 Covers, Happy Self Publishing, etc. I have found that also canva.com is a good option to design a book cover.

8. Give your book a price

Book pricing is at the discretion of the author. The best price range falls between $2.99 to $9.99. For a first-time author, it is recommended to set your book price at $2.99 and gradually add $1 per week.

There is high competitiveness in the book industry with an influx of authors. It then implies that you need a good pricing strategy to be competitive and sell books. Some of these strategies include:

- Consider your competitor's price. Look for the prices of other books in the same niche as yours. This will

help you determine if you can set a higher price for your book.
- Know your fan base. Your fan base determines the changes to make to your book. Famous authors who have extended followers can increase their book pricing. Authors who do not fall in this category should price their books low to attract new readers to purchase their books.
- Book size is a great determining factor in pricing a boon. For instance, you can't charge $50 for a 50-page book. This will turn off customers, even without bothering to assess if the content is worthwhile.
- Measure price by assessing reviews. Positive reviews are a great way to turn visitors into customers. A positive review is social proof or indication that the book has been read and is satisfactory. The higher the reviews received by a book, the higher the pricing. In other words, a book with lower reviews tends to be priced lower than higher reviews.

8.2.5 Tips for success as an author

Tip 1

The first tip is to select a marketable niche that has a large target audience. Various niches are available on the platform - habit development, parenting, camping, or business management, etc.

Tip 2

It is important to write a compelling description. It helps buyers in making purchasing decisions. The description should be personal and empathetic.

Tip 3

Facts and figures attract people. Thus, including numbers, particularly in your subtitle, can be a great way to attract prospective customers to your book.

8.2.6   A few words on the ISBN

ISBN is the abbreviation for "International Standard Book Number". ISBNs are unique identifiers of books. Also, variants of the same book, i.e. Paperbacks, e-books, etc. get another ISBN. E-books published on Amazon (Kindle) do not get an ISBN.

There is an important aspect a with regard to the fact whether your book has an ISBN or not. In Switzerland, for example, in order to get royalties for reprographic rights (distribution for photocopies) your book needs to have an ISBN and if it is self-published (a book-on-demand) it needs to have sold 100 times in Switzerland or has to be taken into the collection of at least three Swiss libraries (source: prolitteris.ch).

8.3 How to make revenue as a software developer

8.3.1 Introduction

Software developers have a variety of revenue models ranging from mobile applications to the Internet of Things, cloud services, and desktop applications. Internet of Things, for instance, has a great potential to deliver a tangible payoff; however, it might not be imminent. Mobile developers target iOS and Android devices.

Developers are essential to the creation of competitive and new products. They proffer solutions to many problems - technical, economic, etc, and people embrace solution-providing apps. Therefore, the more popular a software or an intellectual property is, the more the earning potentials. In other words, software that resonates with the market will make many bucks.

Developers working on desktop apps and cloud service programs make money through royalty payments and software licensing fees. For instance, Microsoft receives royalty payments from computer manufacturers such as HP and Dell to use its Windows operating system on their computers. It also receives royalty payments from smartphone manufacturers such as Nokia to use its operating system on their mobile phones.

8.3.2 Affiliate commissions

Aside from royalties, there are other sources of income for software developers. One of them includes affiliate commissions. There is by recommending some selected products to other stores.

8.3.3 E-commerce

Also, some mobile developers utilize e-commerce (online advertising) as their revenue model.

8.3.4 Subscription service

Another way is to create a subscription service. For instance, a developer who develops a highly demanded software can earn recurring revenue from its license. Users will subscribe to its service to get updates, license code, etc.

8.4 Making money from app development

App developers who are good at coding and can work their way around languages such as Xcode or Unity. The software market, particularly the app development, is becoming lucrative for those who know their onions.

The following steps will help you monetize your skill as an app developer.

1. Register with an app store

Publishing software on app stores such as Apple or Google Play requires you to be a registered member. To sign up to Apple store, you will be required an annual fee of $99. This comes with benefits such as access to testing tools and updated Apple's dev app versions, and the unlimited permission to publish for mobile devices, Mac, Apple TV, Apple Watch, among others.

The sign-on fee to Google Play's development program is $25. It comes with benefits such as access to use Google's online dev tools, Google Payments system for payment acceptance, and in-app payment engines, which allows for the acceptance of money for upgrades from customers.

2. Select a product from a high-demand niche

Before considering developing an app (particularly to generate revenue), it is important to consider the needs of the target market. You wouldn't want to develop an app with little or no marker. Also, you don't want to create an app that is also highly competitive - unless you add certain distinctive and attractive features. A niche to be selected should be one that people are willing to pay for. Competing apps with their price range can be searched on the app stores.

As much as you have knowledge of competing apps, it is also essential to consider apps in the highest-earning categories. IT companies continue to earmark a certain portion of their budget to develop or purchase business and health apps, for instance, to increase productivity as well as keep to terms with the evolving technological development. In other words, businesses, irrespective of the size, are always willing to pay (more) for software that helps them to make money and be more productive.

Though keeping up with the changes in the app development market can be challenging, it is worth investing as the tools and languages, device platforms, and economics continue to witness rapid evolution.

3. Develop a free trial version of the app

People find it very difficult to part with money, especially on a new app that's yet to penetrate the market. They need to ascertain if the software is of high quality and a great benefit to them. For instance, the Super Mario Run developed by Nintendo made a great hit in the mobile game market. It is available for free download and users can play up to three levels. Many users don't know that the full package costs

$9.99 until they have crossed the three levels. Since users found the game - that is, the free versions of the levels - fascinating, they were more than willing to purchase the full package.

Had it been a price tag was placed at the initial level, many users may be discouraged to probe further. The 'free' tag attracted and hooked users before they were requested to pay some amount. They got the experience they expected and continued with the app usage. Even if you will be withholding some features, make them nonessential but nice-to-have. Your hardcore users will cough up more money for more add-on benefits.

4. Use a rating system

Feedbacks are important to any product. They impact the number of downloads you have on your app. No one wants to be the first to use a new product or an innovation. They need to hear testimonies from users who have previously used the app. A higher number of reviews indicate that such a product has a high number of users and visibility. However, it isn't enough to have a high number of reviews, having positive results attributes a great deal of trust for the product.

For apps, there are a variety of rating options that could be used. You can use pop-ups, polite notices, or even slip rating suggestions elsewhere. However, people may have issues with running the app, thereby propelling them to leave behind negative ratings. Thus, it is important to be responsible for the need to fix those issues as they are raised. Make sure to have up to five stars as much as possible - it won't be easy though.

5. Use ads

Thinking it is enough to make money from the app is synonymous with potential limitation. Depending on the type of app you have developed, there are other revenue prospects - hosting ads. Some users use video ads while others use banner ads. To avoid igniting annoying tendencies among users, many developers use banner ads. It consistently displays on the screen, convincing users that making a small in-app purchase can help to get rid of it.

Depending on the suited ads type, it is necessary to sign up with an ad networks. They should be networks that charge decent rates and have easy-to-use tools. For instance, AdMob is a mobile ad network that is owned by Google. It works for both Android and iOS apps.

8.5 How to make money from photo licensing

8.5.1 Introduction

Photos and photographers are in high demand more than ever. This is because large corporations, businesses of various sizes, marketers, publishers, advertisers, bloggers, web and graphic designers buy and use photos regularly online. Pictures of people, foods, tools and equipment, cities, landscapes, nature, etc. are being sought after by online users.

Also, there are now tools that can easily match photos to their respective creators. Thus, the era of stealing photos is fading away. This paves the way for financial prosperity for photographers. They can now safeguard their work, while also earning a stream of income from it.

Just like every art form, photography is an artistic pursuit whose attraction lies in the person's passion and creative abilities, rather than its earning potentials. However, while it may be a hobby, it is also a lucrative profession that could be turned into a career. Many revenue-generating opportunities lie in waiting for photographers.

Even if you don't have a studio of your own yet, you can still make your way around the profession. There are clients that take interest in outdoor or location shoots. Some clients also need photographers to help them commemorate special moments in their lives. People make photoshoots for newborn babies, pre-birthdays, pre-weddings, pets, real estate ads, etc.

To get started, build a strong online portfolio, have a personal website, inform your close associates (that is, friends and family), and utilize the fan base widening potentials of social media and share your works there. Usually, photographers charge a minimum of $100 per session.

8.5.2 Licensing options for photos

To license the photos you have created, as a photographer, it is essential to consider the purpose to which they will be put. If your prospective client aims to use the photos as sales or marketing tools (such as, in a brochure, catalog, or an advertisement), it is necessary to license them for commercial use. However, the use to which they are put are not for profit-making, you may have to grant such clients non-commercial rights.

Another consideration is the exclusivity rights of the photos. For clients who require product photography, photographers can grant such exclusive rights to be used for a specific purpose, time, and geographical location. However, for more generic photos, nonexclusive rights might be the best option as it will create the room for you to resell those licensed photos later.

The third option - first rights - is suitable for photojournalists. It allows for an image to be resold after being used. The image right could also be for one-time use if they only need it for a particular purpose.

Other options are royalty-free or rights-managed agreement, often associated with stock photography. While the former involves a one-time payment for the use of a photo, and not having to pay again for extra uses, the latter involves paying (for a license) to use a photo each time the client intends using it. Royalty-free images can be sold to multiple stock sites.

8.5.3 How to sell image licenses

It is possible to make money off a photo or an image more than once.

8.5.4 Stock photography websites

Stock photography is now home to those willing to sell their products online. You can license your image on stock photography websites who, in turn, sell the rights to use your photos to users such as website and graphic designers and online publishers. It is recommended to study their photo licensing agreement before putting up your photos there.

Stock websites include, among others, Gettyimages, Shutterstock, Alamy, Etsy, Stockcy, iStockphoto, and Dreamstime. Some of these agencies have an equal split with the photographer while others pay on a commission basis.

- **Shutterstock**. Shutterstock is home to over 200 million images, music tracks, and videos for royalty-free purchases. It has millions of purchasing customers. It has paid out over $500 million to its community of contributors across the globe. Shutterstock protects the copyrights of photo owners by granting them ownership credit. As a contributor, you earn each time your content gets downloaded by each customer, and you can make between 20% - 30% on a monthly basis when the payout is usually done.
- **Alamy**. Alamy is a fast-growing stock photo platform. It now boasts as a major contender of Shutterstock and Adobe Stock. Photographers do not require any license or copyrights to upload their photos on the platform. Alamy has made payouts worth $180 million to photographers. It allows photographers to earn up to 50%

on each sale, making it one of the most profitable online stock photo websites to sell photos.

- **Etsy**. Etsy is home to unique handmade goods and boasts of over 30 million users. It has one of the largest audiences and a stable market for purchasing customers. It allows you to sell your prints which, however, have to be packed and shipped. It places price and design setting at the discretion of the photographer.
- You can also create a personal **Flickr** account, upload your photos there, and license them through Getty Images

8.5.5 Your website

Lots of photographers now create their personal websites to sell licensed use of their images. On your website, create an online photography portfolio where you or your work can be easily discovered. Having a personal photo website comes with a lot of benefits - the setting of price and terms of use is based on your discretion, no one takes a portion of your revenue, and you are in total control of activities on it. Many professional photography websites utilize WordPress in their website creation. After creation, you need to display your photos beautifully such that they are attractive and convincing to visitors to make purchases.

8.5.6 Publications and magazines

As a photographer, you can seek publications (both print and online) that would befit your kind of photography, and find out if they need the photos you create. If they need, you can sell licensed photos to them, based on agreement.

8.5.7 Tips to help you when submitting your photos

- Possess necessary property releases to indicate that you are the real owner of the photograph copyright.
- Use your preferred licensing model in line with your area of photography.
- Research and select stock photo agency that has competitive prices, the best commission, and possibly offer discounts.
- Understand the terms of use, submission requirements, and policies well before agreeing to make photo submissions.
- Always consider more than one platform for photo submissions. Rejection is peculiar to the agencies.
- Shoot and submit new work regularly to make your portfolio fresh and up-to-date with market demands.

8.5.8 Other Opportunity: Sell your prints

People are ready to pay for creative works of art (that are of high quality). You can earn some extra money by offering those prints for sale. However, before selling those prints, you require a good printing service (such as AdoramaPix) to ensure a top-notch photo quality. Also, avoid selling photos having people in them as people tend not to buy then. Rather, make the prints what they could easily display in their homes or offices.

Here are a few ways to sell your prints:

- On your photo website or on sites such as ImageKind.
- Display framed copies of the prints at artwork fairs. You can get your purchasing clients there.
- Display your photos at restaurants, coffee shops, parks, or any other outlets where people often gather.
- Offer your clients printed copies directly.
- Local art or photography galleries are also places to sell your photos.

8.5.9 Other Opportunity: Start a niche photography business

You might be versatile as a photographer; however, having a specific niche puts you ahead of other photographers. If you love capturing animals, a pet photography business might be your best bet. If you enjoy traveling, you might fit into travel photography where you take pictures of beautiful sceneries and landscapes. Even if you would be combining several niches, make sure they are related. This increases your credibility, while also building your reputation as an expert in your chosen niche.

For instance, a client who requires the services of a photographer for his wedding will tend to hire a photographer who exclusively specializes in shooting weddings, rather than a pet photographer. As a niche photographer, know your onions and be the best at it. If you make your clients happy and satisfied, they can easily recommend you to their friends.

8.6 How to get paid as an actor for TV shows

8.6.1 Overview

Acting transcends the traditional conception of an actor - one who works in theater, film, and television - and is becoming a vast career field that encompasses web series (such as Netflix and Hulu), commercial TV spots, print modeling, voiceover, training videos (by corporate industries), and hosts for TV and radio shows as well as websites.

Typically, actors do not earn royalties for taking roles in movies or TV shows. Rather, they receive a salary (based on the negotiation agreed upon) after a TV show or movie has been released. They are also paid residuals for the period over which the show or movie generates revenue. In the same vein, actors also get paid some portion of the licensing fees paid by broadcasters each time they air a show or movie on TV.

The actual amount of residuals made by actors depends on the length of the production, the contract signed by the actor, and the medium of production or broadcast. Cable TV, film, and DVD pay varying percentages of licensing fees. Usually, residuals received by actors keep depreciating each time the program airs.

For instance, the initial salary for each of the cast members of the show "Friends" was $1 million per episode while $2,500 was the cap for the first repeat on TV. However, the amount dropped to 40 percent of $2,500 when it was syndicated. Each subsequent repeat continued to witness a decrease. It was until the 13th showing that an indefinite percentage was fixed - 5%. However, this depreciation could be avoided if an appropriate percentage of the gross receipts were negotiated.

Actors in movies or TV shows with a lasting audience will continue to earn a fortune from residuals checks irrespective of their roles - lead or minor.

8.6.2 Payment on contracts

Actors in theater, film, and television may register with the Screen Actors Guild, now SAG-AFTRA through which they are provided the minimum payment rates based on signed contracts.

For daily performers - actors that work on theatrical productions daily - there is a minimum payment of $859 and $504 for high-budget productions and low-budget productions, respectively.

For weekly performers - actors that work on theatrical productions for at least five days in a week - they are paid

$2,979 while those in the low-budget earn between $1,752 and $1,880.

Performers who guarantee availability for production for 10 to 19 weeks receive a minimum of $2,556 each week; and for 20 weeks and above, the earning is placed at a weekly rate of $2,129. For multiple picture performers, they receive up to $2,979 weekly on each movie.

Background actors or extras - those assigned to perform specific skills or activities - earn between $148 and $158. Swimmers and skaters earn $382. Stand-ins for main actors - usually used during light setting or shots focusing - earn $163.

8.6.3 Earning more money as an actor

1. Theater. The theater is becoming a fast-growing industry for actors. It is the purest form of acting. Otherwise known as on-stage performance, it is a platform where actors bring stories to life. It could be on stage or for live audiences. Some film industry hires actors to feature in theatrical plays and musicals both within the country and across the globe. Educational theaters, for instance, go on a regular tour to institutions of learning to create awareness for and sensitize young adults on subjects ranging from juvenile delinquency to women's rights and equity and social justice.

2. Voiceover. The advent of technology has made voiceover become more accessible to screen and stage actors. Actors who have a compelling voice can venture into voiceover. They can create a demo reel. Voiceovers can be lucrative and great side hustles for film and TV acting. As newcomers, you will require a professional voiceover demo. The services of a voiceover actor are required in audiobooks, explainer videos, making documentaries and podcasts, and to act as voice of characters in animated films and video games.

3. Commercials. It is true that the acting style for commercials is different from stage or film acting. The former requires actors to use their acting skills in promoting - and, eventually, selling - a product or service. Advertisers keep looking out for actors with a blend of charm or charisma, energy, and dazzling smiles. Actors in this role could receive handsome reward. They are paid based on the length of time that the commercial runs. For instance, Flo the Progressive Lady has reaped huge rewards on commercial TV spots. The service of a commercial agent might be required to help get auditions. It is also important to understand the terms of the agreement before signing a contract. Otherwise, you might fall into the trap of an unfavorable buyout.

4. Industrial films. Some large corporations make use of actors to play the roles of employees in their corporate

training videos. Usually, the scripts are comedic and realistic, and the themes are centered around the corporate sector. Also, the videos are only circulated internally. The pay is usually excellent and there might be a need to keep bringing the actors as their services are needed. This is a common act among companies such as Chick-fil-A, Home Depot, and Georgia Pacific.

5. Street/live performance. Actors may also utilize their acting skills to earn money by performing on the street or at private events. For instance, musician, magician, or juggler may use their "special skills" in public areas having a lot of foot traffic to earn tip money. Even at theme parks, some firms hire actors to create classic characters for visiting children and their families. Universal Studios and Disney World are good examples of firms that have embraced this act. Large corporate organizations often hold dinners and special events and may require the skill of an actor who can impersonate people.

6. Print modeling. This is distinct from tall, thin people taking a walk on the 'traditional' runway and receiving showers of applause and encomiums. Commercials often utilize lifestyle in print advertisements to sell a product or promote a service. The people used in such ads are actors of different ranges and ages. Actors who have the kind of body structure needed

to model sports clothing are known as fitness models. Other include hair models, shoe models, etc. Sometimes modeling activities may hold at a sales convention, and models feature on catalogs, website banners, posters, and other promotional items or platforms.

8.6.4 How to become a print model

Actors, who have the stamina and charisma required of a model and can equally assemble a catalog of high-quality photographs, can venture into print modeling. The commercial print industry is on a constant lookout for both actors and models (without having a special physical appearance) to feature on the covers and pages of magazines, newspapers, and publications to promote goods and services through advertisements. Large companies such as resorts, casinos, hotels, etc. regularly require fresh faces to advertise their services. The following tips will guide aspiring models in joining the print modeling industry.

- Aspiring print models can visit print agencies' websites to register with them. However, you need to be prepared as most of the agencies are not boot camps for talent development and grooming.
- Actors and models should also get strong, accurate headshot. This reveals your look and personality - features always sought by agencies in prospective print models. You may need to have an online

portfolio with a gallery containing diverse range of images and a variety of looks.
- You should conduct extensive research the market into which you are venturing, to make sure you can capture, for instance, the attention sought by the magazine and newspaper advertisements.
- Read up on pieces of advice from professionals in the industry. You get to learn from their mistakes, learn new trends in the industry, learn modelling gigs, etc.
- Make use of Instagram to network. You can meet new and emerging photographers through the platform. Keep taking photos, meeting people, and receiving feedbacks. You can be walking into limelight through one of your followers.

8.6.5 Tips to becoming a successful commercial actor

- Start taking standup and improv classes.
- Practice regularly in front of a camera, revealing your true nature in front of it.
- Form a group with other actors. You can easily share experiences with one other, read scripts together, practice improv games, see online shows, and even videotape one another. Everything is aimed at skills improvement.
- Watch TV shows and YouTube videos to keep tab on the new trend of style organizers of auditions seek in prospective actors.

8.7 Generating revenue as a fashion designer

Licensing a design idea, for instance, is devoid of the costs and risks usually associated with starting a business. Though earnings from the latter, if successful, can be greater than those of the former, licensing can fetch you a consistent stream of income.

Tips in licensing your design idea

- File a Provisional Patent Application for the design idea.
- Provide written details and a slide deck to potential investors. Be sure to include data obtained from market research, competitive analysis, the status of the patent, cost estimates of the production, and testimonials.
- Ensure the companies have the required manufacturing and distribution capabilities based on their existing retail network.
- Also, follow their protocol before submitting your idea.
- Ask for a guarantee clause to know, for instance, if your idea can be licensed to other manufacturers or the number of units the manufacturer has to sell each quarter or year.

9 Bonus: How to make money on YouTube

9.1 Creating a YouTube channel

YouTube is the largest streaming site that relies heavily on music to drive traffic. The number of your subscribers determines your earning potential on the platform and views, the level of engagement generated, your niche, and the revenue models you explore. To start monetizing your presence or use of YouTube, the following tips will help you.

Step 1 - Create a YouTube channel

YouTube channels are the online presence of individuals on the platform. A channel is attached to each YouTube account, which grants you access to other products and services offered by Google. It allows you to make playlists, upload videos, or comment. You can create a new or existing Google account to create a channel.

To create a channel, visit YouTube.com. Click 'sign in' and sign in using your Google account details. Click on your profile icon and select the Setting icon. Under the 'setting' option, locate "Create a channel" and select it. You then select your desired channel type - personal or business.

Make sure you use keywords that are relevant to the content you will be providing. This will help people locate you easily. Use a short username that people can easily remember.

Step 2 - Add content

Depending on the type of content to upload, upload high-quality content regularly and be consistent with the uploads. Always improve on subsequent uploads. This could be by using a better camera or trying other advanced editing software or methods. People tend to subscribe to channels with a regular upload of content based on a schedule pattern. Create tags for your videos with keywords that are attractive as well ad describe the content. You could be on the track to drive people from YouTube searches to your videos.

Step 3 - Create an establish an audience

Definitely, you need people to watch your ads to increase your earning potentials. Make the best use of social media platforms such as Facebook, Twitter, and Instagram to get subscribers. Even after getting them, you need to keep interacting with them to keep them hooked. This could be by responding to their comments and sometimes, making videos that are directly related to their comments and questions.

Step 4 - Enable monetization on your contents

This includes giving YouTube permission to place ads in your videos. However, copyrighted materials won't fetch you any earning from the platform. To do this, visit www.youtube.com and select "My Channel". Select " Video Manager" and Click channel and Enable on monetization. To start earning, you require a minimum of 1,000 subscribers and 4,000 watch hours. Also, set up a Google AdSense which allows you to earn money per ad click and click.

Once you have monetized those videos online, and have been viewed, you can check out YouTube analytics to see their performance.

9.2 Making money from YouTube music upload

Web entrepreneurs with a wide audience make money on YouTube platform by posting their activities. Musicians, for instance, earn enough from other platforms such as Amazon Prime, Apple Music, or Spotify each time their songs are purchased, played, streamed, or downloaded. However, listening to music on YouTube is takes a slightly different dimension. Google - the owner of YouTube - does not pay royalties to any musician whose songs are posted by users without the musician's permission.

TuneCore - For sound recordings

TuneCore has partnered with YouTube to ensure that royalties are accounted for. The workings of the platform include the following:

- You pay a $10, a one-time setup fee to register all your songs. This covers all original tracks - both current and future - that TuneCore distributes.
- Out of all the sound recordings, select those to be registered with YouTube.
- TuneCore, upon receipt of the tracks, sends them to YouTube, who then registers them in a Content-ID tracking system.
- YouTube conducts a complete catalog search for videos using your music and, consequently, monetizes them on your behalf.
- You then receive your earnings from TuneCore directly to your TuneCore account.

9.3 Selling products or merchandise

There are many products or merchandise from which you can earn money through your YouTube channel. You can manufacture and sell your own products and powering the business through your channel.

Merchandising increases your brand and personality exposure. For instance, you can sell a variety of branded merchandise in your store under a popular brand. When the orders become too much, you can integrate your store with print-on-demand providers.

You can offer discounts to get ahead of other YouTubers.

9.4 Working as an influencer or affiliate

Influencers on YouTube can bring about brand partnerships. Brands are spending a typically large advertising budget on marketing influencers who have gained audience loyalty. The potentials of influencers depend on audience demographics, content quality, and the profitability of their niche.

Some influencer marketplaces offer free products. It is important to utilize opportunities that suit your needs. There are many influencer marketplaces where you can include your channel and increase your visibility to be discovered by big and small brands:

- Grapevine Logic: You only require 1,000 followers to join this popular influencer marketplace.
- Crowdtap: There is no limitation to the number of followers to join. You only require to complete some simple tasks.

Also, you can become an affiliate marketer for brands. This is another way to make residual passive income. You receive commissions from every sale generated through your channel. It is a low-risk venture as payments are only made upon sale. You can include product reviews on your channel. Popular affiliate programs include Amazon's Affiliate network, Clickbank, Share-a-sale and CJ.

9.5 Licensing your contents (videos, news, etc.) to the media

You might have created a funny video clip that had gone viral and captured the attention of a significant number of subscribers on YouTube. It could be licensed to the media in exchange for money. TV news outlets, online news sites, etc. may reach out to you to get the right to use your videos. A marketplace such as Juken Media provides a veritable platform for the right people (target) to locate and purchase your content. Note that the content has to be creative and appeal to the needs of such an outlet.

In August 2019, Facebook reportedly offered to pay $3 million to several news outlets annually in exchange for the rights to license headlines, stories, and article previews in its news section.

10 Misconceptions about royalties

10.1 Myths and misconceptions

Apparent myths and misconceptions often trail royalty payments. This may not be unconnected to the varying laws surrounding the payments across different countries and industries. Setting goals and carer path on these misconceptions amounts to spending time and money to pursue a dream that is far beyond realization. A few industries would be examined here.

10.2 Misconceptions in the music industry

"Publishing royalties are earned from only physical sale of CDs."

There are master recording and composition sides to every music, with each of them earning different royalties. Publishing royalties, which come from mechanical royalties, belong to the composition side. Publishing royalties earned from composition can also be generated from streaming services and video platforms such as Spotify and YouTube, respectively.

"Owning the copyright of a song requires a self-mail."

Owning a song copyright starts at the point of writing the lyrics and chords or simply recording a demo. Once a physical representation can be made, you own the copyright as well as the publishing rights.

"As a songwriters, you can't earn royalties from broadcast (AM/FM) radio."

Typically, songwriters receive performance royalties for broadcast radio. In fact, satellite and some streaming radio services pay out radio broadcast royalties to both sound recording (master) owners and publishers.

"Songwriters sign a publishing deal in exchange to giving up copyright ownership."

This depends on the deal signed. A co-publishing deal agreement implies a signing away current and future songs ownership. To avoid giving up ownership of copyright, it is recommended to have a publishing administration deal. With this, you retain ownership while you are still eligible to earn all future publishing royalties.

10.3 Misconceptions about stock photo royalties

"Royalty-free is the same as microstock and rights managed is the same as premium."

'Rights managed' images may be premium. However, 'Rights Managed' and 'Royalty Free' are simply license models. The do not define whether images are premium or not. Factors that determine the premium qualities of images range from creation of unique imagery to high production value.

"All photos in online public domain is free-for-all."

Copyrights are created to enable creators protect their rights to their intellectual property. Despite the advancement of the internet, creators still have rights of ownership over their creative works. Therefore, to use photos for commercial purposes, you have to acquire its copyrights.

10.4 Misconceptions about book publishing royalties

"You can't make much money from audio books."

Audio books are not without their fanbase. The growing use of smartphone has made automakers such as Honda and GM to integrate audio book apps from iTunes, for instance, in their new models of car. You can time the release of your audio book with those of print and e-book versions. Once the book is suitable for an audio version, you can make a fortune through its release.

"Self-publishing is not lucrative."

How can you make enough money when you only offer your book at a ridiculous price - probably $2.99? This is a common question among critics of self-publishing. As much as there are self-published authors who don't make money, there are equally those that are at the top of the league. Some of them include Adam Croft, John Locke, and Hugh Howey. It all boils down to the story or product and the marketing strategy employed. Once you have an excellent content that will interest people, you can then do an appropriate marketing. However, you require time, money, and energy.

10.5 Misconceptions about oil and gas royalties

"You can't earn much royalties from the industry."

Though oil company industries require intense capital and have the required knowledge and funding for oil and gas exploration, landowners still have much to gain. The company pays for the exploration and extraction as well as purification. These are astronomic costs that will place huge financial implications on landowner if there were to undertake the whole processes themselves.

"Dig deeper for oil and earn more royalties."

Oil occurs in sedimentary rocks and non-petroliferous rocks are encountered at certain depths, below which oil does not exist. The great thicknesses of sedimentary rocks at the depth limit indicates the absence of oil. Only gas exists below that depth, and this is due to the Earth's temperature.

"Property owners earn much quickly."

It is true that oil-rich land may bring great fortune to the landowner. However, it isn't always the situation. For instance, despite the fact that lands having oil running beneath them can be financially productive, it is not every piece of them that yields certain amount of resources. When production pipes are laid, the facilities only select a tiny number of land as worthy. Also, setting off the initial drilling costs may run into years.

10.6 Misconceptions about patents

"Obtaining a patent gives you the right to use other inventions."

A patent only provides the right of exclusivity to prevent others from the making, use or sale of the patented invention rather than granting the permission to use a property. Therefore, possessing a patent does not rule out the possibility of infringing patents of other people. Also, you may be faced with competition from any company and this, if left unchecked, may limit your revenue prospects.

"A provisional patent application is equivalent to a "patent" ."

A provisional patent is only issued to an inventor for a period of one year to allow them verify the market prospects of the invention. It is, therefore, not enforceable by law. The inventor, if they choose to proceed, will then be required to file the patent application. The timing is also essential as it determines whether the patent will be granted or not.

"No more expenses as the patent generates money."

This is not true as there are some extra costs involved. One of such costs is patent maintenance dues, to keep the patent in force. Also, a litigation process may be started against you on the grounds of infringement. This tends to also cost you some money. Contract for royalties may have to be negotiated annually. To forestall likely clampdown on the prospects of your licensed property, you will also have to be on the lookout for parties that (may) infringe upon your patent, whether intentionally or otherwise.

"Ideas that haven't been patented in the past will easily receive a patent."

This is not totally true. It is not every idea that can be patented. The Patent Office might consider such an idea as common knowledge or less useful. There have been many ideas in the past upon which new inventors are only building. Also, some ideas are mere replicates of existing ones. Patents for such ideas would definitely not be granted.

10.7 Misconceptions about licensing

"Internal cloud makes licensing easy."

This may be true to some extent but definitely not to infrastructure managers. Software licensing procedures in the cloud industry come with its challenges though not as great as that of infrastructure and platform. This is because demands in the internal cloud model cannot be predicted, and the procedure may depend on the number of users and the running core of the software. Also, the cloud model team together with the conventional asset manager(s) share the responsibility of software licensing. However, companies with software license control modules may help firms to minimize requirements for hardware and software licensing.

"Buying content is expensive."

It is one thing to buy a content or piece of article and another to license the content. Paying for content creation is customized as it involves paying for someone's intellectual capacity and time. The cost implication of content licensing is far less than that of creating an original content. For instance, an original content might be purchased at the rate of $100 while a similar piece can be licensed for just $20. The advantage of licensing also extends to its versatility. In other words, the party that purchases the licensed content can repackage the content into a variety of forms and distribute across different platforms, as specified in the contract agreement.

"Content licensing is the same as guest posting."

This is also not true. Though both content licensing and guest posting involve featuring someone else's work on another website or blog, there is a thin line of difference. Content licensing simply involves the publishing of a piece of content created by another publisher/author. With that, you select what to feature after paying for the right to use it - in line with the licensing agreement. Guest blogging, on the other hand, usually involves the submission of content by a guest blogger to your site based on your acceptance of such. This is usually done on websites that have wider coverage of visitors. In this case, the aim of the guest blogger is to expand their reach. The only compensation they seek is a backlink (a link that refers site visitors back to their site).

10.8 Misconceptions about copyright

"Online subscription to a journal is a gateway for distribution of contents to other persons."

Copyright owners license contents based on their format or structure and purpose. Thus, distributing such a copyrighted content requires permission from the (original) creator. In some cases, the subscription may allow for internal distribution, that is, distribution within the company. It is quite difficult to come by subscription agreements that allow distribution to individuals outside the organization. Therefore, it is strongly recommended to check the terms of agreement carefully before sending journal contents outside the company. Additional permission or certain payment might be required to do that.

"Most articles allow for contents to be shared on social media sites. Such contents can be used elsewhere without permission."

Contents on public websites are protected by copyright law even if they have a share button option under them. Publishers integrate these article-sharing tools as a business strategy, aimed at making the content gain wider publicity (to social media platforms such as Facbook, Twitter, Telegram, etc.) and bringing traffic (that is, visitors) to their websites. Sharing a copy using other means may require the individual to obtain permission from the owner. This is to avoid any litigation process to be instituted against them.

"As long as the source is cited, I can use third-party content as I like."

Citing a source (author's name, for instance) does not rule out the need to obtain permission or consent from the copyright owner, for use of the content beyond the basic requirements for fair use. The use of more than a few quotes from copyrighted or licensed materials may require you to obtain extra permission or license from agents of (or) copyright owners. Even at that, everything relates to the terms of agreement of use. That is why it is necessary to have prior knowledge of the provisions of agreement to use an intellectual property before using it.

www.ingramcontent.com/pod-product-compliance
Lightning Source LLC
Chambersburg PA
CBHW071421210526
45465CB00001B/483